WHAT IS REGNUM CHRISTI?

A REGNUM CHRISTI ESSAY INTRODUCING THE STATUTES OF THE REGNUM CHRISTI FEDERATION AND THE RULE OF LIFE FOR LAY MEMBERS

FR. JOHN BARTUNEK, LC, STHD

Imprimir Potest
Fr. John Connor, LC
Territorial Director of Regnum Christi
North America
September 5th 2019

Printed in the United States of America

Cover and interior design by Coronation Media

ISBN-13: 9781688564466

TABLE OF CONTENTS

PREFACE — 7

The Nature of the Statutes of
the Regnum Christi Federation and the Rule of Life — 8

The Nature of the Regnum Christi Handbooks — 9

The Usefulness of This Essay — 10

Acknowledgments — 11

INTRODUCTION — 13

A Mission Ever New — 14

A Gift for the Church — 16

A Mysterious Reality — 17

WHO IS IN REGNUM CHRISTI? — 21

IS REGNUM CHRISTI A MOVEMENT OR A FEDERATION? — 25

An Ecclesial Movement — 26

Towards a Change in Canonical Form — 26

One Charism: Multiple Institutions and States of Life — 27

Resolving a Canonical Conundrum — 29

WHAT IS AN ECCLESIAL MOVEMENT? — 31

A New Term for a Perennial Reality — 32

Evangelizing a Secular World — 34

Small Vital Circles of Really Convinced Believers — 36

WHY DO PEOPLE JOIN REGNUM CHRISTI? 41

A Mysterious Resonance 42

Am I Called? 43

Spiritual Affinity and Mysterious Attraction 44

WHAT EXACTLY IS REGNUM CHRISTI'S CHARISM? 47

Charism or Patrimony? 48

Nature: Regnum Christi's Communion 50

Spirit: Regnum Christi's
Experience of Christ 52

Character: Regnum Christi's Style 56

Purpose: Regnum Christi's Mission 59

Transforming Society
with the Gospel 60

Forming Apostles 61

Working with Leaders to Transform Society 62

Working with Leaders: A Multidimensional Concept 65

A Charism: More Than a Slogan 69

HOW IS REGNUM CHRISTI ORGANIZED? 71

Three Levels of Organization: General, Territorial, Local 72

WHAT COMMITMENTS DO PEOPLE MAKE WHEN THEY JOIN REGNUM CHRISTI? 79

A Renewed Christian Commitment 80

The Five Elements of Life in
Regnum Christi 83

Spiritual Life 84

Formation 86

Apostolate 88

Personal and Communal Accompaniment   89

Team Life   91

A Sketch-Portrait of a Regnum Christi Apostle   94

HOW DOES SOMEONE JOIN REGNUM CHRISTI?

HOW DOES SOMEONE JOIN REGNUM
CHRISTI?   97

A Vocation to Be Shared   99

A Vocation to Be Discerned   100

The Act of Association   103

The Continuing Journey   104

Conclusion   106

Appendix: Timeline of Regnum Christi's History   108

More about Regnum Christi   110

PREFACE

The Regnum Christi Federation is the remarkable joining together of individual lay members of Regnum Christi and three consecrated institutions: the Legionaries of Christ, the Consecrated Women of Regnum Christi, and the Lay Consecrated Men of Regnum Christi. Creating this Federation necessitated changes to our previous canonical documents, like statutes and rules of life.

The Statutes of the Regnum Christi Federation, approved on May 31, 2019, are in fact the fourth version of Regnum Christi Statutes. The earlier versions, from 1979, 1988, and 2004, had already undergone various changes as Regnum Christi grew and flourished in different parts of the world.

THE NATURE OF THE STATUTES OF THE REGNUM CHRISTI FEDERATION AND THE RULE OF LIFE

Statutes are a canonical text (canon law is the legal code of the Church) meant to give a Church organization solid and clear structural parameters, which, in turn, help the organization protect and develop its identity in the Church. In other words, Statutes enable organizations to sustain themselves over time and remain faithful to their mission within the Church.

Soon after the approval of the 2019 Statutes, a new type of document was revised and published. Approved by the 2018 Extraordinary General Assembly of Regnum Christi and called *The Rule of Life of the Lay Faithful Associated to the Regnum Christi Federation*, this document applies the common norms of the Federation's Statutes to the state of life of lay members. The Rule of Life is similar to the constitutions of the three consecrated institutions joined together by the Federation. Regnum Christi members from each state of life involved in the Federation need to have a canonical document that applies the common norms in the Federation's Statutes specifically to them. For the lay members, the Rule of Life serves this purpose, though it does not give detailed descriptions of our spirituality and practical guidance, as found in our Regnum Christi handbooks.

THE NATURE OF THE REGNUM CHRISTI HANDBOOKS

Since the first lay members joined Regnum Christi in 1968, we have had a variety of official documents available besides the successive versions of the Statutes: an original handbook on Regnum Christi in 1969; a second handbook in 1971; a third handbook in 1990 (this may be familiar to some current members as the green Regnum Christi manual); and a fourth in 2009, updated in light of the approval of the 2004 Statutes (familiar to some RC members as the little brown handbook). These handbooks contained detailed descriptions of Regnum Christi's spirituality and practical guidance for life in Regnum Christi—something beyond the scope of a legal text such as statutes or a rule of life. Those descriptions and that guidance are needed, and so the newly established Federation will probably set out soon to compose a new Regnum Christi handbook.

THE USEFULNESS OF THIS ESSAY

For current Regnum Christi members in every state of life, as well for inquirers and future members, the Statutes of the Federation are a firm reference point as we journey forward together serving the Church. To that end, *What Is Regnum Christi?* is a short essay that explores the critical concepts found in the Statutes and, by the grace of God, will open new doors for living out the Regnum Christi vocation.

Discussed and revised by an *ad hoc* committee of members from every state of life in Regnum Christi, it is our hope that this Essay will provide, at least in part, a common vocabulary and understanding of life in Regnum Christi that can unify and refresh current members while answering normal and reasonable questions often posed by people inquiring into Regnum Christi.

We recommend that you read this essay with copies of the Statutes and the Rule of Life close at hand.[1] if that isn't possible, then we hope our essay will give enough context to help your understanding. The questions for reflection and discussion interspersed throughout the Essay should make it easy for teams or other small groups to use this document as a springboard for mutually enriching group study and fellowship. Although the different questions addressed in this essay are arranged in a logical order, they do not necessarily need to be read in sequence. Readers should feel free to go directly to the questions most interesting to them.

---

[1]   Both documents are available from the Regnum Christi website. The Statutes are here: https://www.regnumchristi.org/en/wp-content/uploads/2019/06/Statutes-of-the-Regnum-Christi-Federation.pdf, and the Rule of Life is here: https://www.regnumchristi.org/en/wp-content/uploads/2019/06/Rule-of-Life-of-the-Lay-Faithful-Associated-with-Regnum-Christi-2.pdf.

ACKNOWLEDGMENTS

I would like to take this opportunity to thank the members of the ad hoc review committee and my fellow digital missionaries at RCSpirituality.org, who helped make this essay possible: Francisco Gamez, Donna Garrett, Jeff Garrett, Dianne Hart, Michelle Hoffman, Lucy Honner, Deb Levy, Jennifer Meyer, Tammy O'Brien, Fr. John Pietropaoli, Lisa Summers, Rebecca Teti, and Mary Ruth Yao.

INTRODUCTION

For more than two thousand years the Catholic Church has been faithfully evangelizing the fallen world. Evangelizing, in fact, is "the grace and vocation proper to the Church, her deepest identity."[2] Guided, protected, and impelled by the Holy Spirit, the Church has never stopped *proclaiming* the gospel in word and deed, *instructing and initiating* those who welcome that proclamation, and *sanctifying* those who have been instructed and initiated.[3]

And yet, in spite of this two-thousand-year-old-and-counting flow of God's grace, the world still needs to be evangelized. Many people still don't know Christ and need to meet him. Many know him but need to grow in their love for him. And those who love him need to keep following him more and more, with joy, wisdom, and intimacy. As long as this world still contains even one sinner who is not yet a saint, the Church's evangelizing mission must continue—and there are many, many of us sinners who are not yet saints, both outside and inside the Church.

A MISSION EVER NEW

In fact, since the Church "exists in order to evangelize," her work of evangelization will never be complete until Christ comes again to inaugurate the "new heavens and a new earth" (2 Peter 3:13). Every generation must hear the gospel afresh and courageously live it out anew

---

2   St. Paul VI, *Evangelii Nuntiandi*, 8 December 1975, #14.

3   Proclamation, initiation, and sanctification are, in fact, the three primary manifestations or "moments" of evangelization. See *General Directory* for Catechesis, #49, published by the Vatican Congregation for the Clergy in 1971.

amidst the ever-changing challenges and opportunities of human history.

Spiritual and moral progress, the only kind of progress that leads to holiness and true meaning in life, must be vigorously sought and claimed by each individual person and each human community. In our spiritual lives we cannot live off the achievements of the past as we often do when it comes to the material dimension of our lives. As Pope Benedict XVI explained:

> ...[W]e must acknowledge that incremental progress is possible only in the material sphere. Here, amid our growing knowledge of the structure of matter and in the light of ever more advanced inventions, we clearly see continuous progress towards an ever greater mastery of nature. *Yet in the field of ethical awareness and moral decision-making*, there is no similar possibility of accumulation for the simple reason that *man's freedom is always new* and he must always make his decisions anew... Since man always remains free and since his freedom is always fragile, *the kingdom of good will never be definitely established in this world.*[4]

Each period of history poses new challenges to the healthy use of our freedom. And so, God continually revitalizes his Church in her efforts to help successive generations meet those challenges.

---

4   Pope Benedict XVI, *Spe Salvi*, 30 November 2007, #24 (emphasis added).

Regnum Christi must be understood in that context. God never abandons his Church. He constantly stirs up new life within her through his mysterious spiritual gifts, his *charisms*. Regnum Christi is one of those mysterious gifts, "capable of reawakening and nourishing the life of faith of the People of God."[5] As Regnum Christi members, we take our place among many new groups in the Church carrying forward the torch of her evangelizing mission in the here-and-now of human history:

> *Both before and after the Second Vatican Council there arose numerous ecclesial groups that constituted a great source of renewal for the Church and for the urgent pastoral and missionary conversion of all ecclesial life. To the value and richness of all the traditional organizations... are added those more recent realities that can be described as groups of the faithful, ecclesial movements, and new communities.[6]

Though its history spans decades, Regnum Christi is one of those new groups in the Church, a new ecclesial movement, a new community.[7]

---

5   Congregation for the Doctrine of the Faith, *Iuvenescat Ecclesia*, 15 May 2016, #1.

6   Congregation for the Doctrine of the Faith, *Iuvenescat Ecclesia*, 15 May 2016, #2.

7   These are just two of the descriptive, not canonical, terms being used to describe these groups. St. John Paul II explains the core meaning behind various descriptive terms in his 1988 Apostolic Exhortation *Christifideles Laici*, #29.

A MYSTERIOUS REALITY

For many people inside and outside Regnum Christi, the profound crisis sparked by the revelations in 2008 of our founder's scandalous behavior cast doubt on Regnum Christi's future. Could Regnum Christi truly count itself in the company of those new ecclesial groups? Could it be the fruit of a charism given by God to the Church? How could such a gift, they wondered, be given through the agency of an extremely flawed instrument? As the founders of so many other great movements have been made saints, what legacy does Regnum Christi bear with a founder who would not, and could not, ever be a candidate for canonization?

Theologians have wrestled with the *how* and the *why* of that reality, and most likely will continue to do so, but recent events have definitively resolved the what. On May 31, 2019, the Congregation for Institutes of Consecrated Life and Societies of Apostolic Life canonically established the Regnum Christi Federation and approved its Statutes.

Those actions concluded an almost decade-long process of investigation and discernment on the part of the Holy See, and an equally thorough process of reform and renewal among Regnum Christi members. The decree of establishment recognizes that the members of Regnum Christi have indeed received an authentic charism. In this way, the Church is confirming once more that through this charism, Regnum Christi Members embrace and walk on a secure path to pursue holiness. Regnum Christi truly is one of the new ecclesial groups brought into existence through the action of the Holy Spirit, a gift from God meant to benefit the Church and the world. The decree also entrusts the Federation with the task of protecting and developing that charism. Here is the actual text of the decree:

*The Religious Institute of the *Legionaries of Christ*, the Society of Apostolic Life of the *Consecrated Women of Regnum Christi*, and the Society of Apostolic Life of the *Lay Consecrated Men of Regnum Christi*, of pontifical right, whose respective headquarters are located in the Diocese of Rome, have asked the Apostolic See to establish a Federation between them, with a view to safeguarding, deepening, and promoting the common charism; to encouraging collaboration in the apostolate; and to benefiting from a common canonical structure that expresses the unity and fraternal communion of the components of the spiritual family.

This Congregation for Institutes of Consecrated Life and Societies of Apostolic Life, after carefully examining and evaluating each thing, through this Decree, in accordance with canon 582 of the Code of Canon Law, establishes

THE REGNUM CHRISTI FEDERATION.

This same Congregation approves and confirms *ad experimentum* for five years the text of the Statutes of the Federation written in the Spanish language, a copy of which is conserved in its archives.

The canonical form of a federation is new for Regnum Christi. The choice of this new canonical form reflects a more complete understanding of the nature of Regnum Christi itself, fruit of the painful years of crisis and purification. This growing comprehension of our identity and mission is also reflected in the recently approved Rule of Life describing how the lay associated members of Regnum Christi live out our common charism in their state of life.

This essay, *What Is Regnum Christi?*, will explore this maturing vision of our charism as it is expressed in these vital, but concise, documents. It will serve as a useful, though not exhaustive, introduction to these new documents for current Regnum Christi members, and an introduction to Regnum Christi as a whole for inquirers and discerners.

QUESTIONS FOR DISCUSSION:

1. The Church sees new ecclesial groups as gifts meant to renew and revitalize her life and mission in the face of changing circumstances. How do I see them and why?

2. "The kingdom of good will never be definitively established in this world" (Pope Benedict XVI). Why would God send us on a mission of evangelization that we can never completely accomplish?

WHO IS IN REGNUM CHRISTI?

We will explore the meaning and relevance of technical terms like "federation" and "movement" and "charism" later on. But at its most elementary level, Regnum Christi is a group of people. So understanding who those people are is the first step to understanding Regnum Christi.

Catholics in different seasons and states of life are members of Regnum Christi.

1. At the time of the Federation's establishment in 2019, there were approximately 20,000 members of Regnum Christi. Most are adult lay men and women (married and single), reinforcing our identity as one of the Church's new ecclesial movements (a common characteristic of movements is a large lay membership). Diocesan clergy—priests, deacons, and seminarians—can also be members of Regnum Christi. For statistical purposes, they are included in this category.[8]

2. Young people between the ages of eleven and sixteen can also live the Regnum Christi spirit and mission by joining the international youth organization ECYD (this acronym stands for "Encounters, Convictions, Your Decisions"). Here is how the Regnum Christi Statutes describe ECYD:

    > 47. §1. The Federation, in its work for the evangelization and formation of adolescents, directs an organization called ECYD (Encounters, Convictions, Your Decisions), in which adolescents live the charism in a way suited to their age. §2. ECYD is governed by its own statutes.

---

8   Canon law considers diocesan clergy to be "secular" clergy, as opposed to clergy who are members of religious orders.

3. Early on in Regnum Christi's history, some lay members experienced and embraced a call to live our spirit and mission by consecrating their lives to Christ and his Kingdom through sacred bonds (vows) of poverty, chastity, and obedience. These consecrated lay men and women are also members of Regnum Christi. At the time of the Federation's establishment there were about 600 consecrated women and about seventy lay consecrated men in Regnum Christi throughout the world.

4. Finally, priests and religious who are members of the congregation of the Legionaries of Christ are also members of Regnum Christi. In past years, in fact, the Legionaries were sometimes spoken of as the priestly branch of Regnum Christi. Although that term is imprecise and no longer used, it shows how the Legionaries envision the living of their priesthood and religious life—in close union and collaboration with the other Regnum Christi members. As of 2019, there were over 900 Legionary priests and religious worldwide.

ECYD members can become full Regnum Christi members after they turn sixteen years old. Throughout the world at the time of the Federation's establishment there were approximately 11,000 members of ECYD.

Together, these groups of people make up Regnum Christi. Their wide variety of seasons and states of life helps explain why the decree of establishment, the preamble to the Statutes, and the Federation's Statutes themselves all refer to Regnum Christi as a *spiritual family.*

For example:

> [Statutes, #3] The Congregation of the Legionaries of Christ, the Society of Apostolic Life of the Consecrated Women of Regnum Christi, and the Society of Apostolic Life of the Lay Consecrated Men of Regnum Christi, their members and the other faithful individually associated with the Federation, belong to Regnum Christi, a *spiritual family* and apostolic body.

Describing Regnum Christi as a Catholic spiritual family helps express the rich and varied make-up of its membership. Calling it an "apostolic body" indicates that this spiritual family is united in its mission of helping the Church evangelize the world.

QUESTIONS FOR DISCUSSION:

1. What does the term "Catholic spiritual family" stir up in my mind and imagination?

2. How would I describe in my own words the different seasons and states of life represented in Regnum Christi?

IS REGNUM CHRISTI A MOVEMENT OR A FEDERATION?

Simply stated: Regnum Christi is an ecclesial movement whose current canonical form is that of a federation. But what does that mean? Let's find out.

AN ECCLESIAL MOVEMENT

For many decades, Regnum Christi was referred to as an ecclesial movement. The preamble to the Federation's Statutes points this out in its first paragraph:

> Regnum Christi was born *as an ecclesial movement of apostolate* that seeks to make present the Kingdom of Christ through the sanctification of its members and through a personal and communal apostolic action so that Jesus Christ may reign in the hearts of all people and of society. [emphasis added]

Earlier versions of the statutes, versions of the Regnum Christi handbook, and other official documents habitually referred to Regnum Christi as an ecclesial movement. And yet, besides that first paragraph of the preamble, the new Statutes do not mention the phrase. Why not?

TOWARDS A CHANGE IN CANONICAL FORM

With the approved 2019 Statutes, Regnum Christ has changed its canonical form. Canonical form refers to the legal identity of a Catholic organization in the eyes of the Church authorities.

Just as secular legal codes establish different types of legal identities for different kinds of entities (e.g., Limited Liabilities Companies, C corporations, nonprofit organizations), so too does canon law. This is what we mean by the term "canonical form." All movements are required to take on a particular canonical form.

So what happened to the phrase "ecclesial movement"? Though it is broadly used and can be found in papal discourses and in documents published by the various governing congregations of the Holy See, it is currently not precise enough for canon law, and so it does not appear in the Code of Canon Law.

Most ecclesial movements take on the canonical form of an *association of the faithful.* The 2004 Regnum Christi Statutes established Regnum Christi under that same canonical form as an association of the faithful governed by the religious congregation of the Legionaries of Christ.

But there was a problem: ecclesial movements are not generally governed by religious congregations. In fact, most movements do not contain within themselves religious congregations or societies of apostolic life, as Regnum Christi does. The 2004 Statutes, therefore, established an irregular, or at least uncommon, canonical situation.

ONE CHARISM: MULTIPLE INSTITUTIONS AND STATES OF LIFE

The Holy See's investigation and reform of the Legionaries of Christ after the founder's death led to a reevaluation of those 2004 Statutes and a deep reflection on the nature of Regnum Christi as a whole. Members from all states of life participated in that reflection, as individuals and in groups, under the guidance of officials from the Holy See. A greater, fuller, and more nuanced vision of Regnum Christi gradually emerged through that process.

This vision included a realization that the Regnum Christi consecrated women and men required greater autonomy in their formation, mission, and governance. That autonomy was granted during the process of reform and renewal. It was confirmed through the establishment of two Societies of Apostolic Life (another canonical form): the Consecrated Women of Regnum Christi and the Lay Consecrated Men of Regnum Christi. These members, therefore, were no longer to be governed by the Legionaries of Christ.

Concurrent with this new autonomy was a renewed awareness that the religious priests in the Legionaries of Christ saw themselves as *members* of Regnum Christi, even while they were still their own religious congregation. This contradicted the canonical relationship between the Legionaries and the rest of Regnum Christi as the 2004 Statutes had described it. The introduction to the those 2004 Statutes defined Regnum Christi as the specific instrument of apostolate of the Legionaries of Christ, creating a unhealthy separation between the two that has been repaired through establishing the Federation.

The process of reflection and analysis clearly showed that members from all different states of life fully share the same spirit and mission, though each lives it in accordance with their own priestly, consecrated, or secular vocation. In other words, no state of life emerged as either superior or subordinate to the others within Regnum Christi.

RESOLVING A CANONICAL CONUNDRUM

Canonically speaking, we had a conundrum: one religious institute (Legionaries of Christ), two societies of apostolic life (Consecrated Women and Lay Consecrated Men of Regnum Christi), and thousands of individual lay members. What canonical form would—as the decree of establishment puts it—permit all these realities and individuals to "safeguard, deepen, and promote the common charism," encourage "collaboration in the apostolate," and express "the unity and fraternal communion of the components" of our spiritual family? The canonical form of a federation seemed to provide the best solution.[9]

Federations allow autonomous bodies, like religious congregations and societies of apostolic life, to come together in a canonically binding way for a common purpose. A federation also allows for individuals (in our case, the lay members of Regnum Christi) to associate themselves to the federated bodies and so share in that common purpose.

Even though most ecclesial movements have found adequate canonical solidity through the form of an association of the faithful, ours did not. Regnum Christi, therefore, is both an ecclesial movement and a federation. It is an ecclesial movement whose current canonical form is that of a federation?

But what is an ecclesial movement?

---

9   It is worth noting that the Federation was the fruit not only of Regnum Christi members' own discernment, but also of the discernment and guidance of official Church authorities, especially through the assistance provided by our pontifical assistant, Fr. Gianfranco Ghirlanda, SJ.

QUESTIONS FOR DISCUSSION:

1. In my own words, how would I describe what is meant by "canonical form"?

2. In my own words, how would I describe why a federation is a better canonical form for Regnum Christi than an association of the faithful?

WHAT IS AN ECCLESIAL MOVEMENT?

Though it may sound like circular reasoning, the easiest way to get a handle on this term is simply to go back to the concept of a group of people. An ecclesial movement is basically a group of Catholics brought together by the Holy Spirit to help each other live out their own faith more fully and to help further the Church's mission of evangelization.

A NEW TERM FOR A PERENNIAL REALITY

St. John Paul II energetically encouraged the growth of ecclesial movements throughout his twenty-five-year pontificate, believing firmly that they were one of the most beautiful fruits of renewal in the Church after the Second Vatican Council. He offered a succinct description of ecclesial movements, which was referred to again and again in subsequent documents and used almost as a definition by Cardinal Stanisław Ryłko in his introduction to the first official Directory of Associations of the Faithful published by the Holy See.

Basically, St. John Paul II pointed out that "ecclesial movement" is a recent term used to refer to a phenomenon that has been happening in the life of the Church since the beginning:

*And so throughout the Church's history we continually witness the phenomenon of big or small groups of faithful who, through a mysterious motion of the Spirit, were spurred on to spontaneously band together in order to pursue specific goals of charity or holiness in relation to particular needs of the

Church of their time, or even to collaborate in the Church's essential and permanent mission.[10]

Later in that same speech St. John Paul II gives a sketch of how members of these movements make a difference in the life of the Church and the world:

The faithful who gather together in associations and movements, for their part, moved by the Spirit, seek to live out God's word in the concrete reality of their historical circumstances. In this way they become a stimulus, with their own witness, towards a continually renewed spiritual progress, vivifying temporal realities and human values with the gospel and enriching the Church with an infinite and inexhaustible variety of initiatives in the fields of charity and holiness.[11]

In short, every ecclesial movement is like a new plant in the ever-youthful garden of the Church (the word "ecclesial" comes from the Latin word for "church"). It puts its roots deep into the soil of what is essential to Catholic life—sacraments, prayer, faithful doctrine— and blossoms with new manifestations of holiness, virtue, and evangelizing efforts.

In this sense, Regnum Christi fits right into the rest of the new ecclesial movements. As the Statutes put it when describing our ultimate purpose:

---

10 St. John Paul II, *Speech to Ecclesial Movements Gathered for the International Colloquium,* 2 March 1987, #1 (author's translation, emphasis added).

11 St. John Paul II, *Speech to Ecclesial Movements Gathered for the International Colloquium,* 2 March 1987, #2 (author's translation, emphasis added).

7. We seek to give glory to God and make the Kingdom of Christ present in the hearts of all people and in society, by our sanctification in the state and condition of life to which God has called us, and by personal and communal apostolic action.

In many ways, the Church as a whole could say the same thing as that statute: the Church itself exists to give glory to God and make Christ's Kingdom present through promoting both holiness among its members and evangelizing efforts throughout the world.

And that is precisely the point: God continues to raise up new plants in his garden in every generation because as human history unfolds every generation needs to hear and welcome the gospel afresh. Changing historical circumstances require new ways of living and spreading the unchanging gospel, and in our era the new ecclesial movements are part of God's providential care to make that happen.

EVANGELIZING A SECULAR WORLD

Theologians have begun reflecting on why the Holy Spirit raised up these new movements in this particular period of history. No definitive answers can be given, but we can be assured that God knew what a secularized world would look like and the challenges it would pose to Christian life. The new movements, as convinced communities of believers, are able to create pockets of Christian culture in this secular wilderness. They have already shown their power to renew the life of the Church from within and also to magnify Catholic

34

influence in society at large. In his post-synodal apostolic exhortation The Church in America, St. John Paul II even envisioned the movements enhancing the traditional and indispensable life of parishes:

𝒻 One way of renewing parishes, especially urgent for parishes in large cities, might be to *consider the parish as a community of communities and movements*. It seems timely therefore to form ecclesial communities and groups of a size that allows for true human relationships... In such a human context, it will be easier to gather to hear the word of God, to reflect on the range of human problems in the light of this word, and gradually to make responsible decisions inspired by the all-embracing love of Christ. The institution of the parish, thus renewed, can be the source of great hope. It can gather people in community, assist family life, overcome the sense of anonymity, welcome people and help them to be involved in their neighborhood and in society.[12]

In other words, the new ecclesial movements can be considered a kind of preemptive strike made by the Holy Spirit against the increasingly dehumanized social environment of a post-Christian, digitalized culture. Many of the ancient plants in the garden of the Church continue to thrive and bear fruit, but the new conditions in which this garden must grow are requiring new plants as well. This is why St. John Paul II was so encouraged by the new movements and so actively encouraged them:

---

12   St. John Paul II, *Ecclesia in America*, 22 January 1999, #41 (emphasis added).

𝑓They represent *one of the most significant fruits of that springtime in the Church* which was foretold by the Second Vatican Council, but unfortunately has often been hampered by the spread of secularization. Their presence is encouraging because it shows that *this springtime is advancing and revealing the freshness of the Christian experience based on personal encounter with Christ.*[13]

Revealing the "freshness of the Christian experience" by creating havens of authentic Christian culture amidst the "spread of secularization" is one way of describing the Church's mission in this era of human history.

SMALL VITAL CIRCLES OF REALLY CONVINCED BELIEVERS

In that context we can see how the ecclesial movements and new communities fulfill a prediction made by Cardinal Joseph Ratzinger, future Pope Benedict XVI, about what the Church will look like in the coming age:

𝑓The Church, too, as we have already said, will assume different forms. She will be less identified with the great societies, more a minority Church; she will live in small, vital circles of really convinced believers who live their faith. But precisely in this way she will, biblically speaking, become the salt of the earth again.[14]

---

13   St. John Paul II, *Message to World Congress of Ecclesial Movements and New Communities*, 27 May 1998, #2 (emphasis added).

14   Joseph Cardinal Ratzinger, *Salt of the Earth* (San Francisco: Ignatius Press, 1997), 222.

Understanding new ecclesial movements from this perspective of renewal within the Church protects us from making the mistake of thinking that any of these movements or communities—Regnum Christi included—is somehow superior to the Church. The garden of the Church remains the place where all movements thrive. The new plants enrich the garden with their vitality, their beauty, and their fruits, but the garden itself—which creates the environment where the plants can take root and thrive—retains its preeminence.

In this sense, all authentic ecclesial movements and new communities bring a new presentation and manifestation of the gospel—this is the particular gift, or "charism," that the Holy Spirit wants to give the Church through them—but they don't bring a new gospel. St. John Paul II explained this clearly:

> The charism's own originality, which gives life to a movement, neither claims nor could claim to add anything to the richness of the *depositum fidei* [deposit of the faith] safeguarded by the Church with passionate fidelity. Nonetheless, it represents a *powerful support, a moving and convincing reminder* to live the Christian experience fully, with intelligence and creativity.[15]

Our Statutes express this strong sense of being part of the Church and at the service of the Church, as seen in this section describing the spiritual foundations of Regnum Christi:

> 16. We love the Church, the seed and beginning of the Kingdom on earth. We feel we are a living part of

---

15   St. John Paul II, *Message to World Congress of Ecclesial Movements and New Communities*, 27 May 1998, #4 (emphasis added).

her and collaborate in her evangelizing mission. We are loyal to the Pope and the other bishops with love and obedience, know and spread his teachings, back his initiatives and support the local Church.

Movements are meant to support and nourish the Church as a whole, not compete with or supplant her.

The current Directory of International Associations of the Faithful lists 122 associations.[16] (Remember, most movements adopt the canonical from of *an association of the faithful*, whereas Regnum Christi's current canonical form is that of a federation because of the variety of states of life represented in its membership.) Each one has a unique charism. In other words, each one is a particular gift (that is the meaning of the Greek root word behind the term "charism") with which the Holy Spirit has wanted to enrich the Church. But each charism is still rooted in the same soil. Therefore, every ecclesial movement and new community will promote the basic path to holiness shared by every Christian, but they will each promote and live it out in their own, distinctive way.

---

16   Pontifical Council for the Laity, *Directory of International Associations of the Faithful* (accessed 10 July 2019), http://www.vatican.va/roman_curia/pontifical_councils/laity/documents/rc_pc_laity_doc_20051114_associazioni_en.html#PREFACE.

QUESTIONS FOR DISCUSSION:

1. In my own words, how would I describe what is meant by "ecclesial movements"?

2. How might practical difficulties arise between a new ecclesial movement and basic ecclesial structures like parishes? Have I ever experienced such difficulties, and if so, how did I work through them?

WHY DO PEOPLE JOIN REGNUM CHRISTI?

With so many ecclesial movements and new communities in the Church, in addition to the traditional associations of the faithful, third orders, and other parish and diocesan-based groups, why would someone join Regnum Christi?

A MYSTERIOUS RESONANCE

Unlike some decisions, which we make through analysis or t-charts or a study of data, a decision about Regnum Christi touches on something more mysterious.

Every communal charism, as we have seen, is a gift from the Holy Spirit. The people who come together in an ecclesial movement are drawn together by that same Holy Spirit through an attraction, a resonance that they experience when they come into contact with that charism. Regnum Christi isn't merely a decision: it's a supernatural calling, a vocation (the word "vocation" comes from the Latin word for "call"). God invented Regnum Christi, as the Holy See's establishment of the Federation and official recognition of the charism clearly show, and so God also intends some members of the Church to join Regnum Christi and live out in a more specific way—that is, within a specific spiritual family—their general vocation to holiness and mission.

By giving a charism like Regnum Christi to the Church the Holy Spirit is indicating that he will call some Catholics to show in their own lives the gift that Regnum Christi is meant to be for the Church and the world. In doing so, they will also find their own path to Christian fulfillment. A vocation to Regnum Christi brings Catholics deeper into their relationship with God and helps mature their Catholic identity. As St. John Paul II explained:

In this light, the charisms recognized by the Church are *ways to deepen one's knowledge of Christ and to give oneself more generously to him,* while rooting oneself more and more deeply in communion with the entire Christian people. For this reason they deserve attention from every member of the ecclesial community, beginning with the Pastors to whom the care of the particular Churches is entrusted in communion with the Vicar of Christ. Movements can thus make a valuable contribution to the vital dynamics of the one Church founded on Peter in the various local situations.[17]

The many ecclesial movements and new communities inspired in recent decades by the Holy Spirit are meant to enhance the life of the Church and the faithful, not divide or diminish it. God calls people into movements, and into Regnum Christi, because he loves each of us and wants to see his dream for our lives fulfilled.

AM I CALLED?

How do you know if you are one of those people God has prepared to receive the Regnum Christi charism and called to become a saint by helping that charism unfold in your life?

Those whom God calls will feel something stir within their minds and hearts when they come into contact with other people incarnating the same charism. It may

---

17   St. John Paul II, *Message to World Congress of Ecclesial Movements and New Communities,* 27 May 1998, #4 (emphasis added).

not be automatic or immediate. The stirring may come after extended exposure and participation over a long period of time, for example. The *how* and the *when* of a vocation like this may vary from person to person and are part of the mystery of God's loving action in one's life.

At the same time, it is possible to like and appreciate Regnum Christi members, activities, and apostolates without experiencing any internal resonance or sense of heartfelt attraction. Not everyone in the Church is called to join a movement, and not everyone called to join a movement is called to join Regnum Christi—just as not every young man called to the religious life is *ipso facto* called to be a Legionary of Christ.

SPIRITUAL AFFINITY AND MYSTERIOUS ATTRACTION

The interior attraction someone feels to Regnum Christi can show up in various ways. One can feel a need for support and guidance in living out their faith more fruitfully, for example, and find that need met through Regnum Christi activities. Or one can experience an interior desire to follow Christ more radically and spread his Kingdom more decisively, and sense that this desire can be fulfilled by sharing in what Regnum Christi members are doing and experiencing. Each person's path is unique, but if God is calling someone to join Regnum Christi that person's heart will experience, at least to some extent, what St. John Paul II called a "mysterious attraction":

    By their nature, charisms are communicative and give rise to that "*spiritual affinity between persons*"

(Christifideles laici, n. 24) and that friendship in Christ which is the origin of "movements". The passage from the original charism to the movement happens through the *mysterious attraction* that the founder holds for all those who become involved in his spiritual experience. In this way movements officially recognized by ecclesiastical authority offer themselves as forms of self-fulfillment and as reflections of the one Church.[18]

Although the founder of Regnum Christi did not faithfully live out the charism in his own life, the spiritual experience at the heart of the Regnum Christi charism was and is real, and continues to exert the mysterious attraction that builds up the spiritual affinity and friendship in Christ which St. John Paul II described.

A personal experience of that attraction is both a sign that God may be calling someone to join Regnum Christi and a motivation to respond generously to that possible call. Regnum Christi is truly, in this sense, a vocation. As the Rule of Life of the lay members of Regnum Christi puts it in its very first number:

1. The lay members of Regnum Christi are Catholics who, without assuming the evangelical counsels by a sacred bond [i.e., a vow], personally embrace a vocation from God to live their baptismal commitments in the midst of temporal realities according to the charism of Regnum Christi, the fundamental traits of which are described in numbers six to thirty of the Statutes of the Regnum Christi Federation and in this Rule of Life.

---

18   St. John Paul II, *Speech during Meeting with Ecclesial Movements and New Communities*, 30 May 1998, #6 (emphasis added).

This vocation occurs within the context of normal Catholic life and is presented by God as a way to live that life more fully.

Of course, feeling an attraction is not sufficient to discern a vocation to any communal charism, Regnum Christi included. That attraction, or an invitation from a trusted friend or acquaintance, should serve as the beginning of a journey of discovery and discernment on the part of the person who may be called, as well as on the part of the other members of Regnum Christi who are called to welcome in Christ's name those whom the Lord calls into this spiritual family.

QUESTIONS FOR DISCUSSION:

1. [for current Regnum Christi members] When and how did I first experience this mysterious resonance, and how did my response to that unfold?

2. Why is it not always easy to hear God's call in our lives? Why is not always easy to follow God's call even when we hear it?

WHAT EXACTLY IS REGNUM CHRISTI'S CHARISM?

As we have seen, the word *charism* comes up continually in papal and other official Vatican discussions of ecclesial movements and new communities. It is a rich theological term, with many shades of meaning linked to its use in the Bible and in Catholic spiritual writings through the centuries. In our current context, the word charism refers to a core spiritual experience, given and sustained by the Holy Spirit for the good of the whole Church, that brings together and gives life to a movement or new community. The charism is like the DNA of a movement, the origin of the common traits of a spiritual family.

CHARISM OR PATRIMONY?

Like the word *movement* itself, *charism* doesn't appear in the code of canon law. Rather, in the section dedicated to institutes of consecrated life, canon law lists the basic elements of this DNA of a spiritual family using the term *patrimony*. Canon 577 points out that different institutes have different gifts according to the wisdom of God's providential grace:

❝(Can. 577) In the Church there are a great many institutes of consecrated life which have *different gifts according to the grace which has been given them*: they more closely follow Christ who prays, or announces the kingdom of God, or does good to people, or lives with people in the world, yet who always does the will of the Father. [emphasis added]

Canon 578 goes on to link the founding charism of an institute to "the mind and designs" of its founder, and to official ecclesiastical recognition of everything that constitutes an institute's patrimony:

❝(Can. 578) All must observe faithfully the mind and designs of the founders regarding the *nature, purpose, spirit, and character of an institute*, which have been sanctioned by competent ecclesiastical authority, and its sound traditions, all of which constitute the *patrimony* of the same institute. [emphasis added]

The spiritual experience at the heart of a communal charism, therefore, expresses itself in the "nature, purpose, spirit, character, and sound traditions" of that community. Such a rich reality can never be exhaustively defined, as if it were some kind of mathematical formula, but its fundamental traits can be accurately described. This is one of the primary functions of the Statutes of the Regnum Christi Federation. The Federation exists, as the official decree of establishment points out,

❝with a view to safeguarding, deepening, and promoting the common charism; to encouraging collaboration in the apostolate; and to benefiting from a common canonical structure that expresses the unity and fraternal communion of the components of the spiritual family.

In order to do all those things, the Statutes have to express the fundamental traits of the common charism (which you'll find primarily in numbers 6 through 30).

One way to understand the Statutes and the Rule of Life for lay members is to see them as a formal and official description of the "nature, purpose, spirit, and character" of Regnum Christi's common charism (the "sound traditions" that also form part of the patrimony are more practical realities, less in need of canonical expression). Let's consider each of those four terms.

NATURE: REGNUM CHRISTI'S COMMUNION

The nature of something, in canonical terms, refers especially to the specific kind of organization. In our case, Regnum Christi is a federation composed of three institutions (Legionaries of Christ, Consecrated Women, and Lay Consecrated Men) and individual, associated members (lay members). This is described in Part I, Chapter I of the Statutes: *Nature, Composition, and Purposes of the Federation.* Number 6 of the Statutes makes the connection between the *nature* of Regnum Christi and its *spirit* (spirituality) and *purpose* (mission):

> 6. We recognize it as God's plan that the Legionaries of Christ, the Consecrated Women of Regnum Christi, the Lay Consecrated Men of Regnum Christi and the associated faithful live in a profound communion and that we are to be witnesses to the love of Jesus Christ by the unity and charity among us. These institutions, their members, and the associated faithful share a common spirituality and mission, which each lives according to their individual identity and vocation, as expressed in their proper law. This spiritual foundation must inspire and guide the governing bodies of the Federation at its various levels and in the different circumstances of time and place.

The Regnum Christi Federation brings together men and women in different states of life for two general reasons. First, so that together they can help each other live their own lives of grace to the full. This is what is meant by living in a "profound communion" and "being witness to the love of Jesus Christ by the unity and charity among us." Regnum Christi members benefit from the mutually enriching experiences of members in different states of life. We journey together in our pursuit of deeper friendship with Christ, sharing our spiritual experiences and creating a true spiritual family where the giving and receiving of each member creates a multiplying effect. Together we each grow in Christian life more healthily and more quickly.

Second, Regnum Christi brings together members from different states of life to share in a common mission: to multiply the impact of each individual's efforts to build up Christ's Kingdom. The shared spirituality is the bridge between the communion of life within Regnum Christi and the missionary activity reaching out into society. So even though canon law lists nature, spirit, purpose (mission), and character separately, they overlap and complement each other profoundly.

QUESTIONS FOR DISCUSSION:

1. [for current members] How have I benefited from the mutually enriching communion that comes out of the variety of states of life in Regnum Christi?

2. In my own words, how would I describe the "nature" of the Regnum Christi Federation?

SPIRIT: REGNUM CHRISTI'S EXPERIENCE OF CHRIST

In canonical terms, the spirit of a community refers more specifically to a group's *spirituality*, to the aspects of Christ's life and of Christian living emphasized by those who share the grace given to that spiritual family. In Part I, Chapter 2 the Statutes describe the common characteristics of our spirituality, the characteristics shared by members in every season and state of life. But each of the federated institutions also includes a section on our spirituality in their own constitutions. Chapter I of the Rule of Life for lay members (*Identity and Life of the Lay Members of Regnum Christi*) contains an expression of our common spirit and character as it unfolds in the lives of lay men and women.

The Statutes provide the most essential expression of this common spirituality, rich enough to be lived out to the full in so many different states of life. It springs from a heartfelt, personal experience of Christ's love and overflows in an ongoing, ever-deepening friendship with him. That friendship involves sharing both in Christ's love (loving as and what he loves) and in Christ's mission. Number 12 of the Statutes presents this Christ-centered core of Regnum Christi spirituality:

Christ-centeredness

12. Our spirituality is centered above all on Jesus Christ and born from experiencing his love. We seek to respond to our Friend and Lord with a personal, real, passionate and faithful love. Through the action of the Holy Spirit, we are sons and daughters in the Son who becomes the center, standard and model

of our life. We learn to encounter him in the Gospel, the Eucharist, the cross and our neighbor.

No Catholic group or individual would harbor any objections to that statement. In a sense, all Catholics could adopt that expression as their own. After all, every authentic Christian sees Christ as the center of everything. As the Second Vatican Council states it:

*Christ the Lord is the goal of human history, the focal point of the longings of history and of civilization, the center of the human race, the joy of every heart and the fulfillment of all its yearnings. (*Gaudium et Spes*, #45)

But this *Catholicity* of Regnum Christi's Christ-centeredness doesn't detract from its specificity. Every human person has eyes, ears, nose, and a mouth, and yet each person's appearance is still unique. Other spiritual families in the Church, while sharing in the *fact* of Christ-centeredness, would describe their own spirituality in different terms, based on the living of their own charism. St. Francis and St. Dominic would certainly both describe themselves as Christ-centered, but the spirituality of the Franciscans and Dominicans are certainly not identical, nor the same as Regnum Christi's.

Our experience of Christ orients our other devotions: because we have experienced Christ's love and have a desire to love him in return, we want to love all that he loves. Here is how the Statutes describe this orientation of our Marian, ecclesial, and missionary devotions:

14. By revealing the love that burns in his Heart, Christ invites us to love him and all he loves: the Father who

sent him to redeem us; the Blessed Virgin Mary, his Mother and ours; the Church—his Mystical Body—and the Pope; all people, his brothers and sisters, for whom he gave his life; and the spiritual family of Regnum Christi as a way to make his Kingdom present in our hearts and in society.

The following numbers of the Statutes describe how we try to live out those five loves (the Trinity, Mary, the Church and the pope, all people, and Regnum Christi), opening up the horizons of specific *devotions* within the context of our primary *devotion* to Christ and his Kingdom.

Look more closely at that last phrase in number 14. Making Christ's "Kingdom present in our hearts and in society" links our Christ-centered spirituality to our mission. When Regnum Christi members encounter Christ and have a personal experience of his love, their hearts are filled not only with gratitude and joy, but in a special way with a yearning to help spread Christ's Kingdom. The strong, sometimes burning, desire to do something wonderful for Christ, to *change the world* by somehow making it shine more brightly with Christ's wisdom and glory is an aspect of the Christian life highlighted by the Regnum Christi charism. In fact, the words "Regnum Christi" are Latin for "the Kingdom of Christ." The Statutes describe this aspect as our *ideal*:

> 13. Bearing witness to, proclaiming, and expanding the Kingdom of Christ constitutes the ideal that inspires and directs us. Our motto—"Christ our King, thy Kingdom come!"—expresses this longing. Therefore:
>
> > §1. we seek to clothe ourselves with Christ in our hearts and in our works, so he reigns in our lives through a progressive configuration with him;

§2. we let ourselves be permeated by Christ's love for humanity, striving to have him reign in the hearts of all people and society.

Regnum Christi's spirituality emphasizes the commitment to a "progressive configuration" with Christ in the characteristic of *integral formation*—the harmonious development of all the dimensions of the person in the pursuit of Christian maturity:

30. §1. To share a spirit and a mission requires that the formation of all must take into account the characteristic features and requirements of that spirit and mission. This formation must help us discover the full meaning of our lives in Christ, be configured to him, and fulfill our mission. Formation should be integral and include all the dimensions of the person.

Regnum Christi didn't invent the Catholic principle of integral formation—the harmonious development of all the dimensions of the person in the pursuit of Christian maturity—but we have always given particular importance and attention to it.

Our spirituality overflows into an emphasis on certain virtues that equip us for our journey and our mission. Though these virtues are not unique to Regnum Christi, we envision them and combine them in a way that forms a spiritual portrait reflecting the common charism we have received from the Holy Spirit. These virtues are described briefly in numbers 19 through 26 of the Statutes. They include the following: docility to the Holy Spirit; combining a contemplative and evangelizing spirit; a prudent sense of time and its relation to eternity; devotion to the liturgy and the Eucharist; charity expressed especially in hidden service, mercy, and our words; humility and sincerity; and responsibility, emotional stability, and courteousness. Wherever we find a Regnum Christi member, we want to find a deep, well-balanced person capable of making a positive, grace-filled impact in any situation.

QUESTIONS FOR DISCUSSION:

1. [for current members] How has our Christ-centered spirituality affected my own spiritual life?

2. How can Regnum Christi's Christ-centered spirituality be both fully Catholic and also specifically Regnum Christi?

CHARACTER: REGNUM CHRISTI'S STYLE

The spirituality of a community is linked to its character, its particular style of living out the gospel. Number 10 in the Statutes describes this *style* as a "way of self-giving":

10. The personal experience of Christ's love produces an interior urging in our hearts that impels us to passionate self-giving in order to make his Kingdom present: "*caritas Christi urget nos*" ("the love of Christ impels us", 2 Corinthians 5:14). This passion moves us to take on a way of living that is characterized by:

§1. accepting that following Christ includes spiritual combat, the struggle marked by perseverance and trust in the Lord in the face of the reality of evil and sin in one's own life and in society, moved by the power of love to the extreme;

§2. undertaking with a magnanimous, enthusiastic, and creative heart the actions that make the Kingdom present in greater depth and extent;

§3. going out to address the most pressing needs of the world and the Church;

§4. facing challenges with courage and boldness in our personal lives and in the apostolate;

§5. making the most of the opportunities that arise in life to proclaim the love of Christ with Christian audacity;

§6. fulfilling the responsibilities we assumed and striving to give the best of ourselves both in our formation and in our work.

We will see in our discussion of Regnum Christi's mission how we are called to "form apostles" for the Church. When we say "apostles," we mean people who show those characteristics of energy and creativity as they work to build up Christ's Kingdom in their own hearts and in society.

The Rule of Life for lay members describes how this particular character or style—this creative, energetic, and effective approach to living out our Christian identity—is manifested in the lay state of life:

Being an Apostle

9. Lay members of Regnum Christi ardently seek to establish and extend the Kingdom of Christ among all

people. They let themselves be permeated by Christ's charity towards humanity and bring their apostolic zeal to life through intimate contact with him. They long for Christ to conquer their own souls and the souls of all those around them. Impelled by the Holy Spirit and in the style of St. Paul, they endeavor to be supernatural in their aspirations, magnanimous of heart, audacious in self-giving, tenacious in the face of difficulties, and practical and effective in action. They seek to transform the world in Christ. Their motto is, "Christ our King: Thy Kingdom Come!"

This longing to see Christ "conquer their own souls and the souls of all those around them" *characterizes* the life of Regnum Christi members. It is the source of their joyful determination to grow in both the contemplative and the evangelizing dimension of their Christian calling. As the Statutes describe it:

20. We are contemplative and evangelizing:

§1. Contemplative, because we discover Christ's presence and love in our own hearts, in our neighbor and in the world. We seek to be men and women of interior life, lovers of prayer, and we recognize the primacy of God's action in our growth in holiness and in the apostolate;

§2. Evangelizing, because, driven by the desire of Christ to enkindle the fire of the Father's love in all hearts, we live as missionary disciples who seek to proclaim the Kingdom and bring the light of the Gospel to everyone.

Our spirituality overflows in an active, creative, and effective character of following Christ. Where you find a Regnum Christi member, you find a Christian who is willing to go out on the edge for Christ, who is energized by new opportunities to spread his Kingdom in whatever form God presents them, and who will overcome obstacles in order to create and maximize such opportunities even amidst adversity.

QUESTIONS FOR DISCUSSION:

1. [for current members] How have you experienced this "way of self-giving" in your own life as a member of Regnum Christi?

2. What does being "contemplative and evangelizing" mean in one's day-to-day life?

3. What does this phrase from St. Paul say to me personally: "The love of Christ impels us" (2 Corinthians 5:14)?

PURPOSE: REGNUM CHRISTI'S MISSION

Our canonical terms link the purpose—or mission—of a community or spiritual family to the mission of the Church as a whole. We are called to evangelize the world. Christ's last words before ascending into heaven summarize this mission:

*Then Jesus approached and said to them, "All power in heaven and on earth has been given to me. Go, therefore, and make disciples of all nations, baptizing them in the name of the Father, and of the Son, and of the holy Spirit, teaching them to observe all that I have commanded you. And behold, I am with you always, until the end of the age." (Matthew 28:18–20)

Evangelizing, making disciples, requires us to *announce* the gospel, *initiate* those who accept it into Christian living (especially through catechesis and the sacraments), and support the *ongoing growth* of Christians into the fullness of Christ (the work of sanctification, or growth in holiness, or as St. Paul described it "until we all attain…to the extent of the full stature of Christ" [Ephesians 4:13]).[19]

TRANSFORMING SOCIETY WITH THE GOSPEL

As more and more people go through the three stages of evangelization and become mature disciples of Christ, they are moved and equipped by the Holy Spirit to further the Church's work of evangelization in a variety of ways, extending the fruits of their own sanctification into the sanctification of society itself. In this way, the Church grows and fulfills its mission of being like yeast in the dough of the human community,[20] penetrating and transforming the institutions of society (political, economic, and cultural) with Christ's truth. In turn, those

---

19 For these three dimensions of evangelization, see the *General Directory for Catechesis*, #49, published by the Vatican Congregation for the Clergy in 1971.

20 This is one of the ways Jesus described his Kingdom: "He spoke to them another parable. 'The kingdom of heaven is like yeast* that a woman took and mixed with three measures of wheat flour until the whole batch was leavened'" (Matthew 13:33).

institutions better help people live truly fulfilling lives here on earth as they prepare for eternal life in heaven.

This is the mission of the Church as a whole. Every charism born within the Church exists to further this mission in a particular place, through a particular kind of activity—or simply through the renewal of the Church's evangelizing impulse in the lives of the faithful. Therefore, the *overall purpose* of every Catholic spiritual family is the same: to further the evangelizing mission of the Church. When we talk about engaging in "the apostolate" or taking on different types of apostolic activity, we are really talking about furthering that mission.[21]

FORMING APOSTLES

But different groups have different ways of accomplishing that mission. In Regnum Christi, we focus our apostolic activity on the integral formation of new generations of apostles, Christian leaders who enthusiastically and joyfully put their natural talents and influence at the service of Christ in whatever ways the Holy Spirit leads them. And they in turn form other apostles. Here is how the Statutes describe this special emphasis:

Our Mission

8. To fulfill our mission, we seek to make present the mystery of Christ who goes out to people, reveals the love of his heart to them, gathers them together and

---

21   The words "apostolate" and "mission" both come from a root word meaning "to be sent" or "to be sent out." "Apostolate" comes from a Greek root word, and "mission" comes from a Latin root word.

forms them as apostles and Christian leaders, sends them out and accompanies them as they collaborate in the evangelization of people and of society.

Again we see the important connection between our spirituality and our mission. Of all the aspects of Christ's life, the one most central to Regnum Christi is "Christ who goes out to people, reveals the love of his heart to them, gathers them together and forms them as apostles and Christian leaders." Regnum Christi members experience that progressive journey with Christ, and they in turn become messengers and catalysts for others to do so as well.

WORKING WITH LEADERS TO TRANSFORM SOCIETY

Regnum Christi's mission has always included the concept of leadership. To "make disciples of all nations," as Christ commanded his Church to do on the day of his Ascension, requires helping the structures of society reflect Christ's truth more sharply and brightly. Those institutions— from schools, to businesses, to governments, to movie production companies, to orphanages and everything in between—exercise an influence on the "environment" of human society, which can either foster or impede true human flourishing (the "more abundant life" that Jesus came to bring us; see John 10:10). St. John Paul II addressed this important reality in his encyclical on the development of a truly just society:

*In addition to the irrational destruction of the natural environment, we must also mention *the* *more serious destruction of the human environment,* something which is by no means receiving the attention it deserves. Although people are rightly worried—though much less than they should be— about preserving the natural habitats of the various animal species threatened with extinction... *too little effort is made to safeguard the moral conditions for an authentic "human ecology".* Not only has God given the earth to man, who must use it with respect for the original good purpose for which it was given to him, but man too is God's gift to man. He must therefore respect the natural and moral structure with which he has been endowed.[22]

The concept of a "human ecology," of a social environment in which the worldview and behavioral norms promoted by popular culture are either polluting or nourishing the spiritual and moral development of the human community, has been taken up by subsequent popes as well. Pope Francis, for example, quoting his predecessor Pope Benedict XVI, wrote in his encyclical letter *Laudato Si*:

❝ Human ecology also implies another profound reality: the relationship between human life and the moral law, which is inscribed in our nature and is necessary for the creation of a more dignified environment. Pope Benedict XVI spoke of an *"ecology of man"*, based on the fact that *"man too has a nature that he must respect and that he cannot manipulate at will."*[23]

Social structures and institutions, therefore, influence

---

22   St. John Paul II, *Encyclical Letter Centesimus Annus*, 1 May 1991, #38 (emphasis added).

23   Pope Francis, , 24 May 2015, #155 (emphasis added).

the social environment. And so, in order to further the work of evangelization, structures and institutions need to be organized and governed in accordance with Christ's truth. This is done through their *leaders*, individuals who by their natural gifts and by their positions, can exercise exceptional influence over the direction of their structures and institutions. So, evangelization of society includes the evangelization of leaders in all sectors of society. Regnum Christi has always been called to pay close attention to this "existential periphery" (to use another phrase from Pope Francis[24]). Here is how the *Ratio Formationis* of the Legionaries of Christ puts it:

> Besides forming apostles, the Legion works to evangelize those who occupy a place in the public eye due to their position, means, prestige or cultural influence. If these people—who are models for others, shapers of public opinion, and guides of society—turn their hearts to Christ, they have a higher possibility than others have of positively influencing the world in law, the arts, business, education and culture. For the Legion, these people are an "existential periphery" for evangelization. Evangelizing social or economic leaders is not always easy, but it is part of our vocation to bring them to Christ and encourage them to know and put into

---

24 Pope Francis has used this concept in multiple discourses and writings. Here is a clear explanation of what he means by it, taken from a copy of the handwritten text of his speech to the cardinals before he was elected pope: "The church is called to come out of herself and to go to the peripheries, not only geographically, but also the existential peripheries: the mystery of sin, of pain, of injustice, of ignorance and indifference to religion, of intellectual currents and of all misery." From "Havana Prelate Shares Notes from Cardinal Bergoglio's Pre-Conclave Address,"zenit.org (accessed 17 July 2019): https://zenit.org/articles/havana-prelate-shares-notes-from-cardinal-bergoglio-s-pre-conclave-speech/.

practice the Social Doctrine of the Church, and in so doing to transform social structures in accordance with justice and charity.[25]

Special attention to evangelizing societal leaders has been part of the mission of Regnum Christi throughout its existence, though it has never been an exclusive focus, nor has it been a requirement for every single Regnum Christi member.

Let's look now at what the Statutes say about our multidimensional understanding of leadership and what we mean by the formation of Christian leaders.

WORKING WITH LEADERS: A MULTIDIMENSIONAL CONCEPT

In he section explaining the principles that help us pursue our mission and our desire "to make Christ's Kingdom present among us so as to renew society" (Statutes, #32), the Statutes explain four dimensions of what it means to "work with leaders":

Leadership

33. In their mission to form apostles, the members of the federated institutions and the associated faithful:

§1. develop their own leadership, understood as the ability to inspire, guide and form others, and exercise this as a service, following Christ's example;

---

25   *Christus Vita Vestra*, Legion of Christ, Rome, 2017, #96.

§2. through their apostolic activity, seek to help others develop that same ability;

§3. seek to evangelize the persons who bear particular responsibility in the various spheres of life in society;

§4. bear witness to the truth and new life of the Gospel in the exercise of their social duties and their authority, serving the common good with Christian charity.

Each one of us, as a follower of Christ and a sharer in his mission, is called to develop our natural and supernatural gifts. In doing so, we not only experience more fulfillment ourselves, but we also are better able to influence others in a positive way. We help others to know, love, and follow Christ by direct, one-on-one contact (first dimension), and indirectly, through our example and through work that fosters the true good of our communities and of the larger society all around us. Church teaching refers to this as the "temporal realities," as lay people are called in a special way to infuse their world with Christ's grace and truth (fourth dimension).

The second dimension of working with leaders consists simply in helping others develop their natural and supernatural gifts and discover the joy and fulfillment that comes from putting those gifts at the service of Christ's Kingdom. In this sense, Regnum Christi members are effectively working with leaders anytime they are helping others grow humanly and spiritually. We see examples of this as we help ECYD members develop their friendship with Christ or teach the faith to students in a Mano Amiga school for underprivileged children. Helping those individuals develop their gifts and talents, and awakening in them an awareness of their own call to be the "light of the world" (Matthew 5:14), truly is forming new generations of Christian leaders to serve the Church.

The third dimension of working with leaders is that "existential periphery" mentioned earlier: men and women currently occupying positions of particular influence in the different sectors of society. Different members of Regnum Christi will do that in different ways, depending on the possibilities and opportunities offered them by God's providence. The Rule of Life for lay members describes this aspect in the section "Being an Apostle":

9. §4 [the lay members of Regnum Christi] take on their responsibility as lay faithful to bring the light of the Gospel into the public, cultural, economic, political, academic and social arenas of life. They also seek to awaken the apostolic commitment of different kinds of leaders in the world, so they live their ethical and religious convictions more coherently.

The relation between leadership and our mission is also referenced in the concrete commitments made by all Regnum Christi members, as listed in number 17 of the Rule of Life:

17. §4. [The lay member, by associating to the Federation, commits to] apply themselves to their integral formation, and forge their Christian leadership.

In sum, working with leaders is understood as a rich, four-dimensional reality. It is a characteristic expression of Regnum Christi members' love for Christ and their heartfelt desire to answer his call to "give glory to God and make the Kingdom of Christ present in the hearts of all people and in society" (Statutes, #7). In this sense, every Christian is called to develop and exercise influence and leadership in the world for Christ. Everyone can be engaged in this work; it is part of the universal call to mission. St. John Chrysostom described it beautifully in a homily on the Acts of the Apostles:

> Say not, "It is impossible for me to induce others (to become Christians)"—for if you are a Christian, it is impossible but that it should be so. For as the natural properties of things cannot be gainsaid, so it is here: the thing is part of the very nature of the Christian. Do not insult God. To say, that the sun cannot shine, would be to insult Him: to say that a Christian cannot do good, is to insult God, and call Him a liar. For it is easier for the sun not to give heat, nor to shine, than for the Christian not to send forth light: it is easier for the light to be darkness, than for this to be so.[26]

Our multidimensional work with leaders is only one principle that helps us effectively channel our yearning to make Christ's Kingdom present. Other principles include: person-to-person interaction; accompaniment and spiritual direction; formation of formators (people equipped to guide and educate others); scope and depth (choosing activities with maximum scope and maximum depth in favor of evangelization); adaptation to times and places; and organized and effective apostolate. These principles are listed and briefly explained in numbers 32 through 39 of the Statutes. Together they answer the

---

26   St. John Chrysostom, Homily XX on the Acts of the Apostles.

question of *how* we carry out our mission to help the Church evangelize society through forming apostles and leaders. The core idea behind this section of the Statutes is simple: in order to fully *be* Christ's apostles, Regnum Christi members want to develop practical approaches to help *do* apostolic activity effectively.

QUESTIONS FOR DISCUSSION:

1. How can ecclesial movements like Regnum Christi simultaneously share the Church's purpose/mission in general and also pursue their own purpose/mission?

2. Which "mystery of Christ" does Regnum Christi make present in its mission of evangelizing society by forming apostles— Christian leaders at the service of the Church?

3. What does Regnum Christi mean by the phrase "working with leaders"?

4. How does thinking about Regnum Christi's mission make me feel and why?

A CHARISM: MORE THAN A SLOGAN

Having briefly reflected on how the Statutes describe the Regnum Christi charism and explored its nature, spirit, character, and purpose—that is, its communion, experience of Christ, style, and mission—we are better able to grasp just how rich these communal charisms are.

When the Holy Spirit gives a new communal charism to the Church, he is not merely giving a mathematical formula or a new slogan; he is giving birth to a new way of discovering and living out the "boundless riches of Christ" (Ephesians 3:8). This helps us understand why charisms cannot be *defined* in any conventional way, but can be *described*. And the better we get to know them, the better we can describe them.

How can we know the Regnum Christi charism? One way is to have meaningful contact with people who are living it out. Another is to reflect on the various written descriptions that are being organically developed. These include the Statutes themselves, and other official documents like the Rule of Life for lay members and the Constitutions of the consecrated members of the Federation. We can also study the growing collection of Regnum Christi Essays at RCSpirituality.org. One particularly stimulating exploration of the richness of our charism is *The Quest for the Core of the Regnum Christi Charism*, a book written during our years of renewal by two Legionary priests after extensive conversations with members from every state of life throughout the world.[27]

---

27   Owen Kearns, LC, and Patrick Langan, LC, *The Quest for the Core of the Regnum Christi Charism, Second Edition* (Legion of Christ, 2014).

HOW IS REGNUM CHRISTI ORGANIZED?

The Statutes (Chapters 4 through 9) and the Rule of Life for lay members (Chapter 4) describe the organization, structure, and government of Regnum Christi. As a Federation established by the Church, Regnum Christi is required by canon law to provide and abide by certain norms. These norms give clarity and stability to the way its members relate to each other. They guide how we arrange our common activities.

Because they are at the service of protecting and promoting the charism, these organizational norms and structures have changed various times throughout the history of Regnum Christi. They may change again in the future, as the dynamics of the Church and the world change.

THREE LEVELS OF ORGANIZATION: GENERAL, TERRITORIAL, LOCAL

Regnum Christi has three levels of organization: general (worldwide), territorial (which often but not always coincides with national boundaries) and local (a city or a region).

General Directive College

At the general level, Regnum Christi is governed by a general directive college. This consists of the general directors of the three federated institutions (the Legionaries of Christ, the Consecrated Women of Regnum Christi, and the Lay Consecrated Men of Regnum Christi) and two associated lay members who serve as permanent advisors. The president of this college, who represents Regnum Christi to the Church and represents the Federation to all members of Regnum Christi, is by office the general director of the Legionaries of Christ.

General Convention

Every six years, a general convention of Regnum Christi takes place, with representatives from territories all over the world. This is preceded and informed by territorial conventions. These conventions are meant to create space in which the whole Regnum Christi Federation can assess how God is at work among us and where he is leading us, and make necessary adjustments. These conventions also choose the lay associated members who will participate in the general governance for the coming six years.[28]

Territorial Directive College

At the territorial level, Regnum Christi is governed by a territorial directive college. This consists of the territorial directors of the federated institutions present in the territory and associated lay members who serve as permanent advisors.

Plenary Councils

Both the general and territorial directive colleges are assisted by what is called a plenary council. The plenary council at the general level consists of the whole general council of each of the federated institutions plus six associated lay members. The territorial plenary councils follow a similar structure

Regnum Christi Localities

At the local level (a "locality"), Regnum Christi consists primarily of six "sections", each made up of various teams, each team having its own team leader. (When a

---

28   The general convention chooses six lay members who participate in the general plenary council. From those six, the general directive college chooses two lay members to assist the college.

section expands to include a lot of teams, those teams can be subdivided into groups, each with its own group leader.) The six sections are: men's, women's, young men's, young women's, ECYD boys, and ECYD girls. Each section has a director, appointed by the territorial directive college, assisted by a council and a chaplain. Each of the six directors usually participates in the local Regnum Christi council. They are joined on that council by directors of any particularly important apostolic institutions and programs in that locality. This local Regnum Christi council helps orient and coordinate the formation and apostolic activity of all the sections and is usually led by a local Regnum Christi director (RCD), also appointed by the territorial directive college.

A Locality-Centered Federation

At each of these three levels—general, territorial, and local—the various directors and colleges exercise their governing authority primarily in order to provide whatever support and coordination is truly necessary to help promote and protect the charism God has given to the Church in Regnum Christi. The governing structures of the Federation, therefore, seek to enable the members they serve to live the charism to the full, rather than micromanaging life in Regnum Christi. And since members live out Regnum Christi's spirit and mission in the concrete realities of their daily lives, the Statutes envision a locality-centered Federation whose territorial and general structures simply nourish the Spirit-led evangelizing efforts of members in the various localities. Here is how the Statutes describe a Regnum Christi locality:

The locality

54. §1. A locality is a community of apostles and an operative unit of the Federation at the service of evangelization. It covers a geographic area established by the territorial directive college.

§2. A locality promotes communion, coordinates resources and efforts, and fosters the common mission.

§3. The communities of the federated institutions, the sections, the apostolic works, and the apostolic programs all participate in the life and mission of the locality.

§4. The parishes entrusted to the Congregation of the Legionaries of Christ, respecting their proper nature, also interact with the locality.

Some Regnum Christi members live in areas with too few members to form a full-fledged locality. We generally refer to these regions, with maybe just a handful of members or one or two teams, as the diaspora. Members in the diaspora can still live their Regnum Christi vocation to the full, making use of whatever materials and opportunities are available to them, and trusting in the guidance of the Holy Spirit to fill in any gaps.

Here is a basic diagram of the structure of the Regnum Christi Federation:

HOW REGNUM CHRISTI IS ORGANIZED

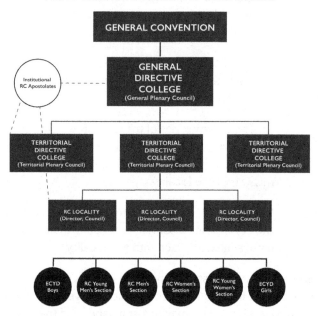

This organizational structure is at the service of Regnum Christi's members and mission. It allows the whole community of Regnum Christi to grow together in Christ, and to support the Church with a broader and deeper evangelizing impact than any of us could have on our own. It also gives each Regnum Christi member a true spiritual family spread throughout the world, wherever we find ourselves. When we encounter another Regnum Christi member we know we have found someone who has been called to serve Christ in the same way we have, with a consistency of spirit and style. Wherever we find another Regnum Christi member, we find family.

QUESTIONS FOR DISCUSSION:

1. Why does an ecclesial movement like Regnum Christi need a governing structure?

2. What do we mean by a "locality-centered" Federation?

3. What is the general role of Regnum Christi's governing authorities?

WHAT COMMITMENTS DO PEOPLE MAKE WHEN THEY JOIN REGNUM CHRISTI?

When God calls us to join Regnum Christi, he stirs up a desire in our hearts to renew and refresh our basic commitment to know, love, and follow Christ as a Catholic Christian. One could say that basic commitment is first made on our behalf by our parents and godparents when we are baptized. Then we make it our own in a special way by choosing to receive the sacrament of confirmation. Joining Regnum Christi,is not an *add on* to that basic commitment but, rather, a renewal of that commitment. Through membership in Regnum Christi, our commitment becomes more *concrete* as we discover a clearer, more personalized path to the fulfillment of our Christian vocation.

A RENEWED CHRISTIAN COMMITMENT

Unfortunately, many outside factors often hinder the development of the grace of baptism and confirmation. We are impaired from bearing abundant fruit in our lives. We do not experience the much-needed transformation into becoming intimate friends with Christ (saints). Personal fulfillment in our faith and the glory our lives should give to God seem distant. We need extra help to shift into a higher, more intentional gear in our Christian lives. That's one reason why the Holy Spirit raises up new movements and communities within the Church. Here it is worth revisiting a statement from St. John Paul II:

❝The charism's own originality, which gives life to a movement, neither claims nor could claim to add anything to the richness of the *depositum fidei* [deposit of the faith] safeguarded by the Church with passionate fidelity. Nonetheless, *it represents a powerful support, a moving and convincing reminder* to live the Christian experience fully, with intelligence and creativity.[29]

And so, at the most fundamental level, through joining Regnum Christi we *recommit* ourselves to a personal and dynamic relationship with Jesus Christ, following him within the Catholic Church. But a new "yes" to God is also added on to the baptismal and confirmational commitment, a "yes" to accepting the gift of Regnum Christi as a *more specific way* to live it out. The communion among Regnum Christi members is a shared spirituality and mission. It is a means and opportunity for growth in holiness and mission, for a new and fuller path of Christian living. Our Christian adventure takes on a specific shape as we make concrete commitments related to the five elements of life in Regnum Christi. Here is how the Rule of Life for lay members puts it:

> 16. The lay member, by associating to the Federation, consciously accepts their baptismal vocation to holiness and apostolate, and gives themselves to Christ so that he may reign in their heart and in society. In this way, they begin a journey of assimilating and living the spirit, communion and mission of Regnum Christi as described in the Statutes of the Regnum Christi Federation, especially through the five elements proper to the life of the lay member of Regnum Christi.

The Rule of Life goes on to summarize the specific commitments made by lay Regnum Christi members. Notice how making these commitments truly renews

---

29   St. John Paul II, *Message to World Congress of Ecclesial Movements and New Communities*, 27 May 1998, #4 (emphasis added).

one's basic commitment to follow Christ, adding to them only a new focus and more conscious intentionality:

The commitments

17. The lay member, by associating to the Federation, commits to:

1. Grow in friendship with Christ, developing the life of grace through prayer and the sacraments;

2. Live the evangelical virtues of poverty, filial obedience, and purity in thought and action;

3. Fulfill the duties of their state of life with love and honesty, as a service to God and to others;

4. Apply themselves to their integral formation, and forge their Christian leadership;

5. Initiate and participate in apostolic initiatives;

6. Profess a faithful and active love for the Holy Church, the Pope, and the other bishops;

7. Generously offer their prayer, talents, time, and material goods to collaborate in the mission of Regnum Christi at the service of the Church.

You can see how these fundamental commitments are aspirational, not quantifiable. None of these commitments is something we can simply check off a to-do list once and for all. For example, we can't quantify "developing the life of grace through prayer," but we can aspire to continued growth in our prayer life. These commitments describe a way of life, a way of Christian living, a path of steady growth that will keep us moving forward in the face of our personal ups and downs, and all the challenges thrown at us in this fallen world.

QUESTIONS FOR DISCUSSION:

1. Why do we need to recommit ourselves to Christ even though we already made that commitment through baptism and confirmation?

2. When I read over a Regnum Christi member's commitments, how does it make me feel? Why?

3. [for current members] Which commitment(s) has (have) been most meaningful to me up to now as I am living out my Regnum Christi vocation?

THE FIVE ELEMENTS OF LIFE IN REGNUM CHRISTI

The path of living our commitments in Regnum Christi is made clear as we engage in what the Rule of Life calls "the five elements proper to the life of the lay member of Regnum Christi" (#16). Here again we see how the Regnum Christi charism is able to help translate the basic elements of Catholic living into a focused, practical reality. The five elements are: 1) spiritual life; 2) formation; 3) apostolate; 4) personal and communal accompaniment; and 5) team life. Each of these elements is described by its own article in the first chapter of the Rule of Life.

Without pretending to be exhaustive, it's worthwhile to consider briefly each of the five elements.

SPIRITUAL LIFE

The spiritual life refers to our relationship with God, rooted in sanctifying grace, which deepens our transforming friendship with Christ and leads us to the fulfillment and fruitfulness we yearn for. As Jesus himself put it: "I came that they might have life, and have it more abundantly" (John 10:10). Here is how the Rule of Life puts it:

> 3. Lay members of Regnum Christi understand the spiritual life as a progressive development of the Trinitarian life within them, which leads to configuration with Christ...

This interior, spiritual growth is primarily the work of God in our souls, but in his loving wisdom he has invited us to be active partners in it. And so, Regnum Christi members consciously help each other to do their part cooperating with the grace of God. The Rule of Life continues:

> 3... Therefore, they live it [the spiritual life] as a dynamic relationship of love with God, nourished by the sacraments, the Word of God, the liturgy, prayer, and the exercise of the moral and theological virtues. Their spiritual life permeates and harmonizes all aspects of their life.

Sacramental life, contact with the Bible, prayer, intentional growth in virtue... These should be part of every Catholic's day-to-day existence; Regnum Christi helps its members make that happen.

Notice how that last sentence from the Rule of Life overlaps the five elements of life in Regnum Christi. Just as the spiritual life "permeates and harmonizes all aspects" of our lives, the other elements also enrich each other with our spiritual life. A team study circle on prayer, for example, may fall under the category of "formation" or "team life", but what we learn there will surely overflow into our own prayerful conversations with God. Spiritual direction is a privileged form of personal accompaniment, an ongoing relationship with someone trained to help others discover and respond to how God is working in their lives. It often sheds light on how we can respond to God—to see what he is doing in our spiritual life, what he is asking of us, and what he is giving to us through our apostolic activity. All five elements are like threads God uses to weave together the tapestry of our Christian lives.

Lay members of Regnum Christi pay special attention to how God works in them and through them in their everyday life as it unfolds in the midst of secular society. This is an essential aspect of the spiritual life for lay people, highlighted in the Rule of Life:

> 4. Conscious of the gift of divine filiation in Christ that they received in baptism, lay members of Regnum Christi live their condition as priest, prophet and king in the midst of temporal realities, aspiring to make the Kingdom of God present in this world so it becomes a worthy home for the children of God in which all things contribute to giving him glory.

This is a manifestation of Christ's call that his followers be "salt of the earth" and "light of the world" (Matthew 5:13, 14).

To stay salty and to keep our light burning—to continue doing our part in the growth of our spiritual life—Regnum Christi members take up certain spiritual disciplines. The most common ones are described in the Regnum Christi prayer book. (These are means for spiritual growth, not ends in themselves.) So the Rule of Life gives us flexibility to personalize these disciplines, encouraging us to use them wisely:

> 5. The spiritual practices recommended to lay members of Regnum Christi are means to help them grow in their relationship of love with Christ. With the help of their spiritual director, they gradually learn mental prayer and how to live the other practices recommended in the Prayer Book. As a privileged means to spiritual progress, it is recommended they participate yearly in spiritual exercises or a triduum [three-day retreat] of renewal.

Spiritual life is the most essential element in the life of every Regnum Christ member, but it is linked to the other four elements as well, supporting them and being supported by them.

FORMATION

Living out our commitments as Regnum Christi members requires us to continue seeking the development of our natural and supernatural gifts. We do this through our own personal efforts, but also together with other Regnum Christi members, With them, we find guidance, materials, and activities specific to our mission. *Anything* we can do to help ourselves keep growing as human beings and as

Catholics falls under the category of "formation." We identify this as one of the five elements, however, because it happens only when we are *intentional* about it. We must make our ongoing formation a personal priority, so that our growth in "wisdom and age and favor before God and man" (how the Gospel describes Jesus in Luke 2:52) becomes a reality and not merely a nebulous desire.

Regnum Christi has always given a privileged place to what official Church documents call "integral formation." We strive to become mature, well-balanced human beings as we pursue the advance of Christ's Kingdom in our hearts and in the world around us. And that means developing all the dimensions of who we are. The Statutes put it like this:

> 30. §1…This formation must help us discover the full meaning of our lives in Christ, be configured to him, and fulfill our mission. Formation should be integral and include all the dimensions of the person.

We also give special attention to deepening our understanding and appreciation of our own Regnum Christi charism, considering it a gift from God for us, a gift meant to be treasured and enjoyed as it blossoms in each Regnum Christi member and community. To quote the Statutes again:

> 18. We love the spiritual family of Regnum Christi as a gift from God that helps us encounter Christ, grow in friendship and intimacy with him, and be his apostles in communion with others… 30.§1. To share a spirit and a mission requires that the formation of all must take into account the characteristic features and requirements of that spirit and mission…

The formation element overlaps with the apostolate because our own deepening formation makes us better witnesses and messengers of Christ. It overlaps with the elements of personal and communal accompaniment, as well as team life, because while our individual hearts take on new disciplines, our true growth is undertaken in the journey we make together, enriching others with our own gifts and being enriched by them in turn.[30]

APOSTOLATE

Earlier, in our discussion of Regnum Christi's mission, we delved deeply into what we mean by our apostolate. Regnum Christi members feel a special resonance with every Christian's call to "Go, therefore, and make disciples of all nations..." (Matthew 28:19). We see ourselves as friends and followers of Christ, and we are especially energized by his generous invitation and willingness for us to be sharers in his own mission of evangelizing the world, making his Kingdom present in every human heart and every human community.

As in the element of formation, Regnum Christi members live out the missionary dimension of their Christian vocation always and everywhere as individuals, but also banding together to support each other to have as great an impact as possible. The history of Regnum Christi, in a certain sense, is the history of its members responding to nudges from the Holy Spirit to come up with creative ways to show the transforming love and grace of Christ to this fallen world.

---

30   Another Regnum Christi Essay is dedicated entirely to this topic: *Our Formation Pathway: A Regnum Christi Essay on Integral Formation and the Journey to Christian Maturity* (RCSpirituality.org, 2019).

PERSONAL AND COMMUNAL ACCOMPANIMENT

Regnum Christi has always had a vibrant belief in Christ's promise that "where two or three are gathered together in my name, there am I in the midst of them" (Matthew 18:20). We value authentic, deep fellowship not only for the mutual support and enjoyment it brings, but also for the many ways it enhances our efforts to spread Christ's Kingdom. Jesus himself made these connections when he prayed for his original Apostles, and us, at the Last Supper:

> I pray not only for them, but also for those who will believe in me through their word, so that they may all be one, as you, Father, are in me and I in you, that they also may be in us, that the world may believe that you sent me. And I have given them the glory you gave me, so that they may be one, as we are one, I in them and you in me, that they may be brought to perfection as one, that the world may know that you sent me, and that you loved them even as you loved me. (John 17:20–23)

Together we make real Christ's desire that his followers "all be one" and live a deep communion with each other in the Lord. This is what we mean by "accompaniment." It is simply journeying together with others, avoiding the Lone Ranger syndrome that has overtaken our fragmented, individualistic culture. The Statutes define accompaniment like this:

> 35.1. Accompaniment is required to form convinced apostles who aspire to the fullness of life in Christ. Accompaniment is understood as close, stable personal

attention marked by selfless service. It seeks to help the other be open to the action of grace and contribute their own human collaboration, so they can respond to the questions and challenges they encounter on their journey of human and spiritual growth.

Accompaniment, like formation and spiritual growth, happens only when we choose to make it happen. We must make space for it, seize the opportunities for it, not only in the most obvious activities, but as a way of life. We *choose* to pursue Christ together with others, leaning on them and letting them lean on us. Regnum Christi seeks to help its members make that choice, and keep on making it. This is why the Rule of Life describes this element in the following way:

11. Accompaniment is a responsibility shared by the lay member, who should seek it, and Regnum Christi, which should offer it…

Spiritual direction is one concrete form of accompaniment. Another is regular, one-on-one dialogue with one's team leader, which becomes a forum for talking about how one's calling to Regnum Christi is unfolding, with its challenges, surprises, and opportunities. The Rule of Life mentions a few other forms as well:

11…This accompaniment is realized especially in personal and sacramental attention, team life, and apostolic formation and follow-up.

Here we see clearly how the fourth element of personal and communal accompaniment overlaps significantly with the fifth element, team life.

TEAM LIFE

The basic unit of life in Regnum Christi is the team, a small group of people (normally five to twelve) usually linked not only by their calling to Regnum Christi, but also by natural ties—they find themselves in the same season of life and in similar social circumstances, with common enough affinities that help them form true friendships with each other in Christ. Here is how the Rule of Life describes a Regnum Christi team:

The Team

14. §1. Lay members of Regnum Christi ordinarily form part of a team. The team is the natural setting where their life in Regnum Christi grows and develops.

§2. A team is a group of members united in Christian fraternity to help each other on their journey of sanctification, in their formation and in their apostolic work, following the example of the first Christian communities.

§3. Teams, as communities of apostles, can be organized in various ways according to the concrete circumstances of each locality of the Federation…

…30.§1. A team is ordinarily composed of members of the same sex and stage of life, bound together by friendship, like-mindedness or common interests. There can also be teams of married couples, directed by one of the couples.

Regnum Christi seeks to offer a true community of Christians, an environment where we each experience

Christ's love for us. This happens not only directly, but also through being known and valued by our companions in the journey and mission we share. For Regnum Christi lay members, the most basic gathering of that community is the team.

The Rule of Life broadly states that team members "help each other on their journey of sanctification, in their formation, and in their apostolic work" without becoming narrowly specific about what that might look like. This reflects one of the apostolic principles mentioned in the Statutes, applying it to our own lives within Regnum Christi:

Adaptation to times and places

38. The members of the federated institutions and the associated faithful, attentive to the needs of the Church and the world and with sincere respect for local cultures, seek to adapt their apostolic activity to the circumstances of time and place, in each case opting for the most suitable methods and forms for evangelization.

Regnum Christi's shared communion, spirit, purpose, and character—especially as expressed in the Statutes and Rule of Life—provide a solid foundation for every member and team, but different teams will adapt the specific activities they engage in according to their "circumstances of time and place." Whatever will help them achieve their purpose as the "natural setting where their life in Regnum Christi grows and develops" is fair game.

The Encounter with Christ
Throughout its history, one particular team activity has fit closely with our charism: the Encounter with Christ. Very early on, the Encounter with Christ took shape and provided

members with a structured but dynamic and flexible way to encourage each other in their Regnum Christi vocation.

The Encounter with Christ is a gathering in which team members reflect on the Gospels, review their Regnum Christi commitments, analyze the events and happenings of their lives in light of Christ's truth, and spawn and develop apostolic ideas.[31] This particular form of fellowship remains a core activity in Regnum Christi. As the Rule of Life puts it:

The Encounter with Christ

15. The Encounter with Christ is the center of team life. In it, the lay members, as a community of faith, by the light of God's Word, examine their Christian life, discern what the Lord expects of them in evangelizing the reality of the world they live in, encourage each other in their following of Christ, and enkindle their apostolic zeal.

In addition, teams traditionally gather for study circles, monthly mini-retreats (these are often offered to entire Regnum Christi sections, with many teams attending simultaneously), apostolic activities, holy hours, and casual meet-ups just for the enjoyment of it. Our hope is that each Regnum Christi team grows to be a "joyful band of missionary disciples," as the Archbishop of Detroit recently put it,[32] modeled on and giving continuity to the very first Christian communities.

---

31   You can learn more about the specific structure of an Encounter with Christ at the Regnum Christi website: www.regnumchristi.org.

32   Archbishop Allen Vigneron, Pastoral Letter *Unleashing the Gospel,* 3 June 2017 (accessed 20 July 2019): https://www.unleashthegospel.org/the-letter/.

A SKETCH-PORTRAIT OF A REGNUM CHRISTI APOSTLE

So, what do Regnum Christi members commit to? They commit to being determined, heartfelt followers of Christ. They commit to pursuing that goal by embracing their call to engage in the five elements of life in Regnum Christi: spiritual life, formation, apostolate, personal and communal accompaniment, and team life. They commit to their journey on a path of deepening friendship with Christ towards what the North American Regnum Christi Territory's Formation Pathway describes as a mature Regnum Christi apostle:

Regnum Christi apostles…

- yearn to continue knowing, loving, and following Christ more and more closely, and therefore actively seek to go deeper in their prayer and sacramental life, to be ever more fully "united to the vine" (cf. John 15:1–10).

- …long to have Christ's grace transform every corner of their being, and therefore also work intentionally on their own human and intellectual development.

- …feel themselves co-responsible for the life of the Church, whose "deepest identity" is evangelizing, who "exists in order to evangelize" (St. Paul VI), and therefore are always ready and willing to reach out to others with the gospel message. They do this through one-on-one encounters, through sanctifying their everyday activities, and especially through creative and organized apostolic action in harmony with their particular state of life in the Church, which for lay people emphasizes transforming the temporal order with the leaven of the gospel.

- …are convinced that Christ's Kingdom here on earth is constantly being opposed by sin and by the "powers of darkness" (Ephesians. 6:12), and therefore seek to live out every aspect of their Christian identity and mission dynamically, with courage, resilience, and astuteness. This is what we have traditionally called a militant spirit.

- …are equally convinced that in Christ the everlasting victory has already been won and given to us through grace, and therefore their lives are marked by a sincere and spontaneous spirit of optimism and joy.

- …have experienced Christ's love for them in a particularly personal way, and therefore give extra attention to passing on that love to others in everything they say and do, especially through hidden acts of kindness and through always showing honor and respect for others in their words. This is what we have traditionally called "benedicencia".[33]

- …view time as one of God's most precious gifts, and therefore seek to use their time wisely and responsibly as a way of glorifying and loving the Lord.

---

33 You can learn more about "benedicencia" in the RC Essay Sharpening Your Tongue: A Regnum Christi Essay on Charity in Our Words, available at RCSpirituality.org.

QUESTIONS FOR DISCUSSION:

1. Which of the five elements is naturally most attractive to me and why? Which is least attractive and why?

2. [for current members] Which of the five elements has been strongest in my Regnum Christi experience so far and why? Which has been weakest and why?

3. Which of the five elements needs more attention in my life right now and what can I do this week to give it more attention?

HOW DOES SOMEONE JOIN REGNUM CHRISTI?

The Rule of Life points out that the decision to join Regnum Christi should be a mature decision, the fruit of a healthy, patient process of discovering and discerning one's call. The decision takes concrete form in a person's written request for association, submitted to the relevant section director along with the informed recommendation of a team leader or another member of Regnum Christi. Here is how the Rule of Life describes this process:

Process:

20. §1. The decision to request association to the Federation must be the fruit of proper discernment and a free response to the call of God.

§2. Admission is the responsibility of the section director, and can be granted in response to a written request by the person interested in associating, with the recommendation of the team leader or another member, after a period of participation in the life of Regnum Christi long enough to ensure that both the person and the section director have come to know each other sufficiently.

§3. Association takes place, ordinarily after a spiritual triduum, through a formal act or ceremony as established in the Rites of Regnum Christi, which must express what is established in numbers 16 [spiritual significance of the act of association] and 17 [commitments] of this Rule of Life. The association is registered in an official record.

§4. Lay members make an annual devotional renewal of the commitments they acquired at their association.

The process of "proper discernment" takes place between someone's initial contact with or inquiry into Regnum Christi and their decision to request membership. The Rule of Life describes this discernment as "a period of participation in the life of Regnum Christi long enough to ensure that both the person and the section director have come to know each other sufficiently." Such a patient, intentional approach to joining Regnum Christi flows from our awareness of Regnum Christi as a true charism given by God to the Church. People who join Regnum Christi are responding to a call from God to live this charism, for their own good and for the good of the Church and the world. And hearing and heeding a call from God is not always easy.

A VOCATION TO BE SHARED

This reality of Regnum Christi as a calling, a vocation, is at the root of Regnum Christi members' efforts to share with others what they have found in this charism. When we meet someone who seems to have a resonance or potential resonance with our spirit and mission, we can respectfully speak to that person about Regnum Christi and invite them to participate in and learn more about it. We all long to share the Catholic faith with those who have not yet accepted it, because we care about their salvation. In a similar way, we want to share our experience of Regnum Christi with those who may have a Regnum Christi vocation. We know that if God is calling them to Regnum Christi, they will find there the path to a deeper and more fruitful relationship with Christ. The Rule of Life describes this attitude in its section on "Being an apostle":

9. Lay members of Regnum Christi ardently seek to establish and extend the Kingdom of Christ among all people. They let themselves be permeated by Christ's charity towards humanity and bring their apostolic zeal to life through intimate contact with him. They long for Christ to conquer their own souls and the souls of all those around them… Therefore, the lay members of Regnum Christi:…

> …§7. desire to share with others the gift of God they have discovered in Regnum Christi. So they introduce and invite others to Regnum Christi, and accompany those who show an interest in getting to know it, or in participating in its spirituality and mission.

A VOCATION TO BE DISCERNED

The path of discernment between initial contact and actual membership involves a "free response to the call of God" (Rule of Life, #20). If such a call is present, it can take many different forms, but discernment usually involves at least three steps or stages:

1. Initial contact with Regnum Christi. This can come through family members who are in Regnum Christi, through some kind of apostolic activity organized and carried out by Regnum Christi members, through friendship or acquaintanceship with Regnum Christi members, through formation materials produced by members of Regnum Christi, or through participation in some kind of formation activity organized by Regnum Christi members. Sometimes this initial

contact results in an immediate experience of deep resonance. Other times it sparks curiosity or simply provides a person with something they find useful and encouraging for their lives, and in that way stirs up a desire for further contact.

2. Ongoing participation in Regnum Christi. This also can take many different forms. Some people are deeply attracted to an RC apostolic activity or institution (e.g., missions, schools, or youth ministries), and their Regnum Christi journey really takes off as they become more and more involved in that work of evangelization. Others find consistent, satisfying spiritual nourishment in Regnum Christi retreats, spiritual direction, evenings or mornings of reflection, holy hours, or other formation activities. Regular participation in these can gradually stir up an awareness of an interior resonance with the Regnum Christi charism that could indicate a divine call. For others, the participation is more personal, taking place simply through a growing friendship with one or a few Regnum Christi members. In these friendships, a person gradually becomes aware of a desire to share more deeply in the spirit and mission they see at work in their friends' lives. Whatever form it takes, ongoing participation in Regnum Christi is necessary for a call to mature.

3. Formal discernment of a vocation to Regnum Christi. A confirmed awareness of resonance with the Regnum Christi charism will, eventually, lead a person to ask the question: Is God inviting me to become a Regnum Christi member? At that point, the discernment process becomes more intentional. Most Regnum Christi sections or localities offer

what is traditionally called a "discernment course" for people in this stage. This course creates space for interactive explanations and discussions of the kinds of questions we have been examining in this essay. Discernment courses are often done in small groups and provide inquirers with a forum for asking questions and getting to know other experienced Regnum Christi members. Usually the person in charge of the discernment course will also be available for more one-on-one conversations, which are also essential for a healthy discernment.

Along with participating in a discernment course, this period of formal discernment should also include some kind of participation—even if only occasional—in a Regnum Christi team, since team life is the basic platform for the other elements of life in Regnum Christi. Some people will be able to discern and decide very soon after, or even in the midst of, a discernment course. For others, it may take longer.

Once someone discerns a call to Regnum Christi and decides to embrace it, they request permission to become a member through something the Statutes call a "formal act or ceremony of association."[34]

---

34   This is specified in #20 of the Rule of Life for Associated Lay Members. It is worth noting that many members of the federated institutions (the Legionaries of Christ, the Consecrated Women of Regnum Christi, and the Lay Consecrated Men of Regnum Christi) started their journeys as members of ECYD or as lay Regnum Christi members. Lay members associate individually to the Federation in order to become members of Regnum Christi., whereas members of the federated institutions join Regnum Christi through the collective institutional membership of their institution.

THE ACT OF ASSOCIATION

The ceremony of association usually takes place after a three-day retreat (triduum) which serves as a spiritual preparation for this important step and for the beginning of one's life as a Regnum Christi member. (Members devotionally renew their "yes" to their vocation on an annual basis, often at the conclusion of their yearly triduum of renewal.)

At this point, they are welcomed by a team and they begin their journey as a Regnum Christi apostle, living out the five elements of life in Regnum Christi as a way of fulfilling their commitments and responding to God's call in their heart. Usually new members will be offered some initial instruction and formation specifically designed to help establish a strong and complete foundation for a fruitful life in the Movement. These, in fact, are the first two phases of formation in Regnum Christi: Discernment and Initial Formation. (The next two phases are Core Formation and Ongoing Formation.[35])

QUESTIONS FOR DISCUSSION:

1. What could be some indications that someone is called to Regnum Christi?

2. How would I describe in my own words the three steps or stages of discerning a call to Regnum Christi?

---

35   You can learn more about the phases of formation for Regnum Christi members in the RC Essay *Our Formation Pathway*, or by visiting RCSpirituality.org (accessed 21 July 2019): https://rcspirituality.org/formation-pathway/.

3. [for current members] What do I remember most vividly about the process through which I discovered, discerned, and decided to follow my Regnum Christi vocation?

THE CONTINUING JOURNEY

Since the Regnum Christi Federation is a large, widespread, and complex reality, it will always need some of its members to serve the spiritual family from within. Spiritual directors, team leaders, section directors, locality directors, apostolate directors, and other functions necessary to keep the spiritual family healthy need to be lovingly carried out by qualified members. These kinds of behind-the-scenes functions can be undertaken by members for a specific period of time. But they can also become a kind of calling within one's call to Regnum Christi, an ongoing apostolate, a way of embracing God's invitation to make present the Kingdom of Christ. Many Legionaries of Christ and consecrated women and men of Regnum Christi live out their vocations in this way, serving the rest of the spiritual family as their primary field of missionary activity.

For some lay members, responding to a call like this takes the form of a special "promise of self-giving." The Rule of Life describes this promise in detail in Chapter 3, with the first section giving an initial glimpse of this beautiful dimension of life in Regnum Christi:

Article 1. The promise of self-giving

24. §1. Some lay members feel called by God to take on a special commitment of self-giving and availability

to the Lord in order to promote the life and mission of Regnum Christi. In response, they undertake the journey of prayer and formation that Regnum Christi proposes to them, and they commit to active involvement in Regnum Christi with their prayers, talents, time and material goods.

§2. Those who accept this call offer valuable support to the sections and their apostolates through their prayer, self-giving and availability.

§3. The lay member of Regnum Christi and the section director agree on the concrete ways of living out this self-giving and availability according to the member's personal circumstances and Regnum Christi's needs.

§4. It is the responsibility of the lay member of Regnum Christi to harmonize this commitment with the duties proper to their state in life, aided by their spiritual director.

The essence of the promise of self-giving is spiritual, a response to an interior call to take on a "special commitment" to preserve and promote this spiritual family. In a similar way, other Regnum Christi members may feel an interior call from the Lord to take on a special commitment to a particular kind of apostolic activity. In other words, this promise doesn't create a super-class of especially holy Regnum Christi members, but rather offers an avenue through which God provides for the sustenance and support of the spiritual family of Regnum Christi.

It is worth mentioning at this point that even though Regnum Christi is a true vocation, in and of itself it is not a state in life, like marriage or consecrated life. Consequently, as the Rule of Life explains, lay members are free to disassociate from the Federation at any time, hopefully after "having reflected before God about their decision" (Rule of Life, #21.1).

CONCLUSION

We began this Essay with the question, What Is Regnum Christi? By now, you can see why the answer needed more than a sound bite, a paragraph, or a single page. As the gift of a new, communal charism to the Church, Regnum Christi is a rich, multifaceted reality. It is a group of people in various states of life gathered together by the Holy Spirit to help renew the Church through a dynamic, Christ-centered spirituality that emphasizes the evangelization of individuals and society through creative and effective apostolic action.

If you want to learn more, or find a Regnum Christi member near you, contact us through our website at regnumchristi.org.

APPENDIX: TIMELINE OF REGNUM CHRISTI'S HISTORY

1941	Foundation of the Legionaries of Christ
1963	The term "Regnum Christi" is first used to describe lay members of the spiritual family in an initial draft of the Statutes
1968	The first lay people associate (at the time it was called "incorporation") to Regnum Christi
1969	The Foundation of the Consecrated Women of Regnum Christi
1970	ECYD begins
1971	The second Regnum Christi Handbook is published
1972	The Foundation of the Lay Consecrated Men of Regnum Christi

The first lay members make their promise of self-giving (called at the time incorporation into the second degree of Regnum Christi) |
| **1979** | Publication of the first internal Statutes of Regnum Christi |

1988	First revision of the internal Statutes of Regnum Christi
1990	Third edition of the Regnum Christi Handbook is published.
2004	Holy See's approval of the Statutes of Regnum Christi
2008	Death of Marcial Maciel, LC, founder of Regnum Christi, and ultimate exposure of his deplorable practices
2009	Apostolic Visitation of the Legionaries of Christ and Regnum Christi, followed by period of reform and renewal under the guidance of Papal Delegate Cardinal Velasio de Paolis
2014	Approval of the revised Constitutions of the Legionaries of Christ
2018	Establishment of the Lay Consecrated Men of Regnum Christi as a Society of Apostolic Life
	Establishment of the Consecrated Women of Regnum Christi as a Society of Apostolic Life
2019	Establishment of the Regnum Christi Federation and approval of its Statutes

MORE ABOUT REGNUM CHRISTI

To continue learning more about Regnum Christi, you may be interested in our growing collection of Regnum Christi Essays (extended, in-depth reflections on particular aspects of life as a Regnum Christi member)

SHARPENING YOUR TONGUE

UNTIL CHRIST BE FORMED IN YOU

OUR FORMATION PATHWAY

See all the RC Essays and other great Catholic resources at RCSpirituality.org

Made in the USA
Las Vegas, NV
14 September 2023

77574176R00066